Bringing Out the Best in You

Nicole Harvey

Photograph by Christopher Hawkins

I0087130

© 2011, Nicole Harvey

ISBN: 978-0-578-09944-6

Dedication

I dedicate this book to the loves of my life Ne'Kole and Ny'Shaun, my precious daughters. If it was not for these two precious jewels, I probably would have given up a long time ago; but I am still fighting to show them the other side that God has in store. Where there is milk and honey. I have to make my dreams become reality for the both of you. Momma loves you ladies deeply!

My second dedication goes out to the lady that inspired me all my life, my lovely grandmother. Thank you for walking many of my dark roads with me. The many times I've cried in your ear (I'm giving up) you will say you are my grandchild and giving up is not in us. You will tell me keep fighting lil girl. I love you so much for that and you are the reason I'm able to show my children about God and show them a better life. My love for you grandma is unexplainable.

Last but not least, this dedication goes to the man of my life. Thanks for being supportive in all I do; you have been amazing for standing by my side with all I've ever wanted to do. Thank you, love your wife.

Contents

DON'T MAKE EXCUSES/MAKE IT HAPPEN

I grew up in a single parent home with only two siblings; however, every niece and nephew my mother had was always at our house and this left little time being spent with us. I did not grow up in a perfect home. We moved each year and changed schools constantly, which were very unstable for my siblings and I.

When I was younger I was never taught how to love nor did I grow up telling my siblings I loved them; however, my brother and I did establish a very strong bond at a young age and now that we are older my sister and I have become closer than ever. My mother's heart has always been as big as this city, so I do not want to point a finger at her because she gave us everything in the world as far as "materialistic", but the one important thing we needed the most she failed to give because she did not know how to love. Needless to say, I grew up to learn my mom could only give us what she knew.

See, my mom became pregnant with me when she was merely a teenager, so I suppose she missed her childhood and chose to live it out later in her life by partying all the time. My mom probably went out at least four times a week and I even remember some of the clubs she went to like the Flamingo, Rose, Polynesia Room, Garrets, and the Living Room just to name a few.

Unfortunately, I became a teen mom as well and this forced me to grow up faster than I should have. Therefore, I did not experience a normal adolescence and the thought of hanging with my friends and having fun was all over. By the time I was seventeen I had my own apartment and by eighteen I had been introduced to all of the government assistance programs that were available to a young mother. I received section 8 benefits and lived off of it for a few years. However, I quickly realized that this was not the life I want to live. I wanted something different than what I had been exposed to all my life because everybody I knew received some type of government assistance. Consequently, I was told I would never make it without the assistance.

Although, I received negative feedback I wanted a different life for my daughter, so eventually I decided to walk away from all of the free things. Moreover, if you find yourself in a situation where you need to use government assistance please use it as a stepping stone in order to better yourself. In my opinion, waiting for two hundred dollars a month is for the birds and is not worth depending on because you can work for what you want.

Thankfully, my grandmother kept all of my cousins, the neighbor kids, and I in church when I was young and she talked to us all the time about God and for us to experience a better life. This was very impactful for me because my mom and I did not have a great relationship when I was young and I was always told that I would never amount to anything. I was called out of my name and talked bad about to every friend of mine and hers. My mom also spoke about me negatively to our family.

Throughout the years, I let those words eat me alive, but later realized the things she said to me and about me were untrue. Those words only kept me in bondage and unable to move forward in my life. At this point in my life, I had given birth to my second child and I was so determined to make something happen in my life. Even though I did not have a college education I did have God and once you find out he is all you have you learn quickly he is all you need! Needless to say, I decided to start a daycare and once I put that thought in my head I turned in my resignation and trusted God. When I started my daycare I did not have any money, but I believed that I could make this dream come true.

Before, I started my daycare I was working at Barnes Hospital and made a little less than twenty thousand a year. Once I started my daycare it took me two years to exceed that income. By the fourth year I had more than tripled my annual income. It was a great feeling to earn an income of that magnitude.

After, accomplishing my dream about six months later, I had planned it out in my head. I knew that no matter what negative things you have been told, names you have been called, or how small you may think of yourself you are worthy of any and everything you want to accomplish in your life. God promised you an abundant life right here on earth. Know who you are and whose you are because you are a child of God. I believe you can and will be all God created you to be. So, when nobody else understands the vision and passion you possess trust that God is looking down saying my child step out on faith because I will never leave nor forsake you.

For instance, my brother, Stan wants to make it in the music industry. He tried and tried, but seemed to get nothing accomplished here in

St. Louis. Stan thought long and hard about relocating where there might be a better chance for him to pursue his dream. Stan did not want to leave his family or me especially. Our family had never been separated before. All of our lives, we have been within arms reach of each other and at this time Stan was indecisive about the move. In a new city he would not know anyone there and was afraid of being all alone. When he performed in his hometown he knew he would have his family to cheer him on, but if he left who would he have?

After months of thinking things over my brother finally asked me what I thought he should do. Remember my brother and I have a very close relationship, so naturally I did not want him to leave. However, once I thought it over, I decided to tell him to go pursue his dream. Sometimes we have to let go and move on to get where we want to go. He found a place in a new state and we drove nine and a half hours to see the place and it was very nice, which at that time Stan decided he would accept the place and two months later we packed him up and drove Stan to Atlanta in order for him to pursue his dream.

The day we had to leave him there was the worst feeling in the world, but there is so much opportunity there for him. It is normal for him now to walk out the door and run into a celebrity riding down the street, walking in the mall, or even sitting next to one at a restaurant. He has had so many performances there already and he has only been there for a year.

Even though, he was without his supporters he would walk into different venues and perform. Performing has become easier because the feedback he has received. The positive response has been so great; it pushes him to keep going. Not long after he arrived, he met so many people whom he was able to get studio time and find more places to perform. He is so close to his dream, closer than he has ever been before. Stan did not make an excuse he made it happen!

What I am saying to you is DON'T MAKE EXCUSES MAKE IT HAPPEN! Whatever your dreams are please go after them. It does not matter what color, size, education, or upbringing is. I want you to know you can do all things through Christ who strengthens you (Philippians 4:13). I cannot tell you the sky is the limit when there are footprints on the moon. If you fall, get back up and try again. The only failure would be not trying at all. God said He knows the plan He has for you. The plan is for you to prosper and give you hope and a future (Jeremiah 29:11).

When you begin pursuing your dream, one thing I do not want you to do is despise small beginnings. What may look like a little to you can be a whole lot to someone else that is watching. Always take time to write things down that come to your head and never let a thought just pass you by. The only person in this world that can hold you back is YOU, so get out of your own way. I hope to inspire you to move to the next level in life.

My lovely daughter wants to be a pediatrician yet she is starting to complain about the eight years of school. I tell her it is only eight years of school and you still will be so young. At twenty six years old you will have completed medical school and will begin your successful career. I do not think you can beat that and believe it will be worth each year spent to accomplish her dream.

Whatever it is you want to do please do it and do it NOW. Do not try to find the easy way out because you will find yourself doing the same thing over and over again. I have friends that have been in school for over twenty years because their dream was to be a doctor, but settled for a nurse and now they keep going back. So when you know what it is that you want pursue it no matter what it takes. Anything worth having is worth fighting for. This is why I am telling my lovely daughter "DON'T MAKE EXCUSES MAKE IT HAPPEN!" I will see you in ten years walking across that stage receiving that PHD.

For example, a young lady by the name of Sharrell was born in St. Louis, Missouri and moved to Indiana in 1997 with her family. She graduated high school and enrolled at Indiana University in Bloomington, Indiana in 2006. During Sharrell's high school and college life she and her family experienced some great hardships. The greatest one was when Sharrell was coming home for the summer of 2008. Her mom had lost her job, her car, and her apartment. They had been evicted. With no other option Sharrell & her sister had to return to St. Louis and live with family until things were better.

Stressing about her family's situation it was hard for her to focus on school. But God is good if you trust Him. Their family got back on their feet and Sharrell went back to school stress free for the time being. With one year left of college Sharrell's mom decided to move back to St. Louis leaving her alone in Indiana to finish school. Despite all the obstacles in her life, Sharrell graduated from Indiana University with a degree in Athletic Training. She could have dwelled on being left there alone, but she made a choice to finish what she started. She wanted a life without struggle and she knew that in order to do that she could not make EXCUSES she had to make it HAPPEN.

If you dropped out of school it is not too late to get up and go enroll back in and if you can not go back to high school enroll into a GED program and start there. Once you are done there and you want to pursue your college education go right ahead and do whatever you want. Nothing shall stop you from pursuing your dreams, and you know we DON'T MAKE EXCUSES WE MAKE IT HAPPPEN! It is worth it because it is no fun living life every day doing something you dislike. Look at each day as an opportunity to push closer and closer to your dream. When you see yourself at the top there is no better feeling than knowing you did it. So let's get going and I'll see you at the top!

In a failing world there is no such thing as a perfect family. Our children have many needs: physical needs (food, shelter, and clothing); emotional needs (love, acceptance, affirmation); intellectual needs (the opportunity to learn daily living skills and to develop intellectually); and spiritual needs (guidance in how to know God personally and to mature in that relationship). However, dysfunctional families have common patterns like not speaking to one another, keeping family secrets, ignoring inappropriate behavior as well as altered perceptions of reality, they do not feel in order to disregard legitimate emotions, they do not trust and live in isolation to avoid more broken promises, children strive desperately to be perfect trying to meet all the parental expectations.

Such families are shaped by impaired parents who consistently distort or deny reality to conceal their own problems such as: workaholic or abusive behavior (addictive, sexual, physical, and emotional). The result in a child's life is shame, a deep sense of inadequacy and worthlessness, and the burden of unmet unrealistic parental expectations. The good thing is the Lord desires to be the "Repairer of the breach" for families in which children have been maligned or afflicted! So please be sure to remember that no matter what type of upbringing you experienced we do not MAKE EXCUSES WE MAKE IT HAPPEN!

NOTES: How can I make it happen?

Goals_____

_____

_____

_____

Sunday_____

_____

_____

_____

Monday_____

_____

_____

_____

_____

Tuesday_____

_____

_____

_____

_____

Wednesday_____

_____

_____

_____

_____

Thursday_____

_____

_____

_____

_____

Friday_____

_____

_____

_____

_____

Saturday_____

_____

_____

_____

Accomplishments_____

_____

_____

_____

USE YOUR RESOURCES/OPPORTUNITIES

As young adults we often think we know everything and do not need help or anyone to guide us in the right direction, but later on in life we find out that is not the case. We wish we could go back to that person who tried to tell us what was right and wrong. We wish we could have written that essay that lead to a scholarship. I have seen so many children sit back and not take advantage of the resources of someone who cared. It may not be a family member or a close friend, but it is other people out there that care about your well being. I ask you please never disrespect those that come out to give their time and information to better your life.

I have personally sat in schools and watched children talk while someone was providing very helpful information to them. You have to understand that they already have what they need in life, but they are trying to help you get where you need to be. While you are in school there are social workers and counselor available which you can go to for so many different reasons like assistance for your personal needs to family needs.

Resources come in many different forms. Your parents, grandparents, friends, organizations, school, pastors, leadership programs, mentors, and books are all considered very good resources. I know we sometimes do not like to read, but you will find it very helpful. Do not be afraid to ask for help and never feel like the others that believe they are to cool to ask for help or even listen to someone for advice. I will suggest a mentor because there is nothing wrong with having someone in your life that cares for you and are willing to help you.

A young lady I know, Jami, had been successfully going through school with a 4.0 and is about to graduate now. She enrolled in school on a big loan and a small grant and had various resources that would help her to accomplish her goals and get help to eliminate the debt of her loans. She told me that she wished she had used those resources because debt is a very serious issue and loans are even more serious. She had many chances at reducing her debt while still attending college. The school offered career services, scholarship info, weekly employment packets and a lot of resources and resourceful people. She told me that she regretted not taking advantage of those opportunities while in school, but it is not too late to work on it. After, accepting and understanding all of her mistakes she said that all students no matter what level should use their resources because there is a lot of support out there, but you just have to be willing to do some real research and ask for help sometimes.

I have had plenty of opportunities in my life that I let pass me by not knowing until later that I missed those opportunities because I chose not to use the resources that were available to me. Some of the reasons I missed those opportunity was because I thought I had it all together and other times pride stood in the way because I did not want to ask a particular person a question or maybe even listen to that person. In some cases I even thought I could not do whatever it was I needed to do. Pride is the worst thing you could have. Pride goes before destruction, so know if you have a pride issue please get rid of it NOW!

God gave each of us different passions, so that everything he wants done in this world will be completed. If you are unsure of where you going, there is a chance that you will end up somewhere other than your proposed destination. For example, Ne'Kole runs track and at one of her track meets a scout watched her and decided he wanted her to run track for them in the summer. He came up to her and presented her with his card, so she could contact him to start running in his summer program.

He saw the best athletes while he sat back and watched; however, the rest was left up to Ne'Kole. After, she decided to reply she later found out that at least 90% of the organizations children receive full scholarships. What an opportunity that would have been to miss. Either receive a full scholarship or spend a number of years after graduating paying for student loans. Don't miss out on your opportunity by failing to use your resources.

Ny'Shaun wanted to sing in the choir, but she was unsure because she did not know what others will think about her singing. Later she decided to try out for the choir and was chosen to be apart of it. This year Ny'Shaun and her choir attended Holiday World, which was located in Indiana where there were over fifty choirs that attended. Out of fifty choirs Ny'Shaun's choir won 1st place.

If she would have missed that opportunity she would not have been apart of the choir's success. Ny'Shaun did not make an EXCUSE she made it HAPPEN. Ny'Shaun also had an opportunity to be in a fashion show at Church on the Rock, but she declined the offer and after a few days she decided to take the fashion show coordinator up on the offer. Once the fashion show was over Ny'Shaun said it was the best feeling in the world. That fashion show made her a more confident person. Go after each and every good thing that comes to your mind. You are the only one that can stop you from where you destined to be. Do not be afraid because God did not give you a spirit of fear, but of power, love, and a sound mind.

CREDIT CARDS & COLLEGE STUDENTS DON'T MIX

College is a time for students to expand their minds, meet new people, and have tons of fun. However, it can also be a time when a student can get into serious financial trouble courtesy of easily-accessible credit cards.

BUILD CREDIT:

If handled properly credit cards have a lot to teach college students. Those who use them and always pay their balance on time will build a solid credit history and boost their credit score. This will be great when you graduate, land that first job, and look to buy a new car or home. Nothing looks better to a lender then paying your bills on time.

CROSSING A DANGEROUS LINE:

Unfortunately, this easily-accessible line of credit often proves too tempting for many students. They max out their cards and then are shocked to see the resulting sky-high minimum monthly payments. To avoid this problem a student should keep a relatively low credit limit of no more than $1,000 once he or she has a proven track record. Know that this limit could be increased over time, but make sure good spending and payments habits are instilled before raising that credit limit.

SHOP 'TIL YOU DROP THE RATE:

You also need to be a better shopper before you get a credit card. Most student credit cards include rates that are higher than the average rates for typical cards. They may also offer low introductory rates, which eventually adjust to more than twenty percent after the temporary period has ended. The fallout can be high minimum payments, which may eventually trigger equally painful late fees.

Like anything else in adulthood privilege comes with great responsibility in using credit cards wisely. I want you to prepare for a solid financial future. It is an invaluable lesson in money management that most schools do not offer you all, but you all need to know desperately.

I have had one of the top credit scores and I have had a low credit score as well. When my credit was at its highest point, I was able to walk on any car lot and drive away with a vehicle without putting any money down. I was able to purchase homes with no money down. I had plenty of credit cards from major cards to department stores to gas cards. You could not tell me anything all I needed was an ink pen and I had what I wanted. They smiled when I walk in and they pulled my credit. I am talking about homes well over a hundred thousand dollars and cars and trucks starting at thirty thousand dollars. I did not even need check stubs when I went to the car dealership because my score was so high. Little did I know I was set up for failure.

At that time you could not tell me anything. I thought I had it all under control. Little by little and day by day, I lost all of those great things I had. I drowned in debt. It did not matter to the creditors how good I paid before or how many years I had already paid. On some items I only had a few payments left. I was treated like crap when the creditors called. Was it worth it? No, because it felt like it only took overnight to tear my credit down and years to build it back up.

So, I am a witness. Do not go buying things just because you can. Get what you need until you can afford what you want. I have learned and I will not purchase a car now unless I can pay cash for it. Instead of buying a brand new car get a slightly used one until you can afford a brand new one.

There is nothing wrong with having what you want just make sure it is the right timing for it. I love all the finer things life has to offer, but I had to learn when the right time was for what I wanted. Unfortunately, I had to learn the hard way and I want you to learn from my mistakes, so you do not have to put in all the extra work. Your credit is very important so please protect it.

NOTES: What resources/opportunities can I take advantage of?

Goals_____

_____

_____

_____

Sunday_____

_____

_____

_____

Monday_____

_____

_____

_____

_____

Tuesday_____

_____

_____

_____

_____

Wednesday_____

_____

_____

_____

_____

Thursday_____

_____

_____

_____

_____

Friday_____

_____

_____

_____

_____

Saturday_____

_____

_____

_____

Accomplishments_____

_____

_____

_____

NOTES: What resources/opportunities can I take advantage of?

Goals_____

_____

_____

_____

Sunday_____

_____

_____

_____

Monday_____

_____

_____

_____

_____

Tuesday_____

_____

_____

_____

_____

Wednesday_____

_____

_____

_____

_____

Thursday_____

_____

_____

_____

_____

Friday_____

_____

_____

_____

_____

Saturday_____

_____

_____

_____

Accomplishments_____

_____

_____

_____

THE POWER OF WORDS

We all should know how powerful our words are. Maybe you have heard the saying, "life and death is in the power of the tongue" **(Prov. 18:21)**. That quote is so true and today we are where we are because of the words we spoke years ago. We set our words into motion. We activate them by speaking. When we speak we do one or two things: speak faith filled words or fear filled words. The power of words is not theory it is a fact.

We are supposed to imitate God, but in order to do that we are to talk like him and act like him. Matthew 17:20 says because of our unbelief for assuredly I say to you, if you have faith as a mustard seed, you will say to the mountain, move from here to there, and it will move; and nothing will be impossible for you. He would not ask us to do something that we are not capable of doing.

Faith words activates the power, and when you believe in the power of God's word it activates faith, and when we speak faith filled words out of our mouth they will have the power to change any situation we may have. Faith is like the key that you turn to activate the engine of your vehicle. You have the fastest, prettiest, toughest, and most powerful automobile on Earth, but if you do not have the key, the power to the automobile will not benefit you.

Without faith to turn the power of his word on, you cannot experience the power of the word. When the word is not mixed with faith it produces no profit **(Hebrew 4:2)**. Faith makes the word of God profitable. Concrete has no value if you do not add water, but if you add water you can build the foundation for homes, bridges, buildings, and many other things. If you are not profiting off the word then I will have to question whether or not you are reading your bible. Your words are to be spoken with power and along with that you have to believe that you have what it says you can have.

Many have spoken words without qualifying them with faith and then when these words did not come to pass they got discouraged. To speak the word without faith is to speak the word without the necessary equipment to activate the power and see the results in your life. When you have taken the time to read and put the word in your heart by confessing the word then your faith you have in your heart will activate the power on the words spoken.

Believing and speaking will override the natural laws:

David did not defeat Goliath with his slingshot and with his rock; he defeated Goliath with his believing and speaking (1 Samuel 1:7)

The three Hebrew children believed and spoke what they believed and what they spoke came to pass in their lives (Daniel 3)

The woman with the issue of blood kept saying what she believed and what she said is what she got. I am not sure she believed it first, but she kept saying it and all of a sudden faith was provided in her heart and she had what she said (Mark 5:28).

Jairus believed and he said if you touch her she will live and that is what he got. The opportunity came to say something else when the evil report came, but he exercised the vocabulary of silence and did not say anything to negate his confession and he had what he said (Mark 5:22).

Joshua, God heard the voice of a man, Joshua believed and he spoke and had what he said (Joshua 10:12-14)

Jesus did not pray to God he spoke to the storm and he had what he said (Mark 4:35)

Abraham, he did not call what was, he called what was not and he called it into being (Roman 4:17)

We are spirit beings and when we speak words of faith from our spirits we can change physical things.

Everything physical you can see was created by God who is a spirit that you can not see (Hebrews 11.3). God who is a spirit created all matter by speaking words out of his mouth (John 4:24, Genesis 1)

Physical things that we can see.

A spirit made all matter so all matter is subject to a spirit.

A spirit gave birth to the physical.

The creator is never subject to the creation.

Everything physical is subject to the spiritual God created man in his own image of himself.

The Heart-Mouth Connection whatever is in your mouth is going to produce an image in your heart and whatever image you have in your heart is going to come out of your mouth in words and create your life.

The things you have placed inside your heart have been coming out of your mouth and determining your life (Matt 12: 33-37).

You are bringing forth the things in your life by the words that you believe in your heart and speak out of your mouth. The words that are coming out of your mouth are results of what you have deposited in your heart you are saying it because you believe it. According to Jesus, what you believe and what you say will determine what you bring forth in life. By your words you are made right or freed and by your words you can be condemned.

I want you to understand that it is okay to prosper. It is okay to have money. It is ok to have a nice home and car. It is ok to pay your bills on time. It is okay to be debt free. It is okay to have beautiful clothes. It is okay to have the desires of your heart. That is part of being God's child and having an inheritance from God.

Jesus said he came that you might have "more"! He came that we might have "more" what is more? It is more than you have right now. More than what is in your closet. More than what is in your house. More than what is in your refrigerator. More than what is in your garage or in front of your house. More than what is in your bank account. YOU SHOULD BE SHOUTING RIGHT NOW!

You have to have information because God does not bless ignorance. And you need to have information on the word of God, as well as information on whatever business, vocation or whatever area God is going to bless you in. You are going to have to do what it takes. You are going to have to use your brain more than ever.

In order to receive the wealth that is waiting on you; you must first renew your mind with God's word. You can not go continue blaming each situation and others. You will have to take responsibility. You must say no to lack, fear, hate, envy, jealousy, sickness and disease.

Some people believe they can be rich if they just knew the right people. I want you know it is not who you know, but it is what you know. If you know and stand on the word of God you will have the abundance Jesus proclaimed regardless of who you know. God will place the most qualified people into your life that will help assist you in fulfilling your current plans or goals. The knowledge of God's word comes first.

The first and most important key to having more is being knowledgeable. God's people are destroyed because of the lack of knowledge they possess (Hoses 4:6). Knowledge is power as it can save your life. Knowledge gives you an advantage over the competition for a job. Being knowledgeable allows you to make money.

Doctors, lawyers, engineers, and other successful people make more money than regular jobs is because of what they know. The knowledge they have acquired is what makes them more valuable; however, the most valuable knowledge is spiritual knowledge.

God wants you to have the knowledge of his word which is life changing, practical, and spiritual knowledge. This will give you success, prosperity, and a better life! The devil does not want you to know more. Satan wants God's people ignorant of spiritual truth and ignorant of the inheritance they have in God. In John 10:10

where Jesus said he came that we might have more.

The thief came only to steal, kill, and destroy. The devil tries to keep you from having more. The devil tries to steal knowledge from people by preventing them from learning, discovering, and getting revelations from God's word. That is the main way Satan steals from people and keeps them in poverty and lack! If the devil can keep you ignorant of the word of God he can keep from having a "sword" to defeat him!

Ignorance of the word of God is one of the primary reasons people experience the lack of peace, lack of joy, lack of health, lack of success, lack of victory, and the lack of prosperity in their lives. A wise man is strong and a man of knowledge increases his strength. (Proverbs 24:5)

People normally want to achieve many things in life, but wisdom is the key principle; therefore, you need to obtain knowledge and wisdom first!

Since power lies within one's tongue you should speak positive words more often. This is one of the main secrets to success and riches. This means you need to speak God's word over any and all situations and circumstances in your life. Moreover, you need to be careful when you speak because you do not want to speak negative words about your circumstances which will be contrary to God's Word.

Keep your eyes on your dream and you will keep correcting, adjusting, forgiving yourself, and forgiving others. Maybe you need to go to college or maybe you need to get out of the job you are currently in and find a better job, but please do not quit the job you have before you find the other job. Begin speaking more faith filled words out of your mouth, have faith in God, take appropriate action, and start watching God's riches begin to grow in your life!

NOTES: Everyday I need to change my words.

Goals_____

_____

_____

_____

Sunday_____

_____

_____

_____

Monday_____

_____

_____

_____

_____

Tuesday_____

_____

_____

_____

_____

Wednesday_____

_____

_____

_____

_____

Thursday_____

_____

_____

_____

_____

Friday_____

_____

_____

_____

_____

Saturday_____

_____

_____

_____

Accomplishments_____

_____

_____

_____

<u>Birds of the feather flock together</u>

The old phrase "Birds of the feather flock together" means you are known by the company you keep. Therefore, hang around good people and people will believe you are a good person as well and vice-versa. When you hang with negative people others will associate you with being a negative person.

I am very particular about whom I spend my time with because my time is precious and I can not get that time back nor do I have any to waste. I know that the people I hang out with will eventually rub off on me whether good or bad. I am a person that likes to care for others and tries new business ventures, so I try to associate with people who are already fulfilling and/or working towards fulfilling their dreams. I like being around people who has much more knowledge than me. This gives me the ability to always have someone there that I can learn from, as well as continue climbing higher and higher.

This may come as a surprise to you, but it is not such a wise decision to be the smartest person in your circle because it leaves no room for growth. You will have no one to learn from and everyone else will be pulling from you. Always be open to meeting new people, so you will not be stuck at a stand still. Step out and attend different events in the area. Go alone to the events sometimes because when we have people with us that we are comfortable with we tend to socialize less with others we do not know because we already are in good company.

Find friends who like enjoying some of the same things you enjoy and have friends that have no problems celebrating you when needed. A friend should be able to tell you congratulations to all your accomplishments and remember important days like your birthday without you having to tell them.

A true friend would love to see you do well even if they are not. No matter how hard it is a true friend will encourage you to do right even if it cause some disagreement you will later realize they were right. If your friend acts different towards you when they are around others or if you have a friend that has a nasty attitude for no apparent reason get rid of them because it will eventually rub off on you. Stay away from the one who always wants to be the spotlight because you should all shine together. Do not allow anyone to pull the life out of you and you definitely do not want friends who compare themselves to you.

If you have a friend that tries to pressure you into doing things that is not right or is jealous of you then let them go as fast as you can

and do not look back because that so called
friend means you no good.

NOTES: What company I need to keep or delete.

Goals_____

_____

_____

_____

Sunday_____

_____

_____

_____

Monday_____

_____

_____

_____

_____

Tuesday_____

_____

_____

_____

_____

Wednesday_____

_____

_____

_____

_____

Thursday_____

_____

_____

_____

_____

Friday_____

_____

_____

_____

_____

Saturday_____

_____

_____

_____

Accomplishments_____

_____

_____

_____

The Value of Goals

How many times have people asked you, "What do you want to be when you grow up?" This ambiguous question leaves some children dreaming of being the first astronaut to take a horse into space or open an ice cream shop, while other children are left in a mild state of frozen panic because they can not imagine ever growing old enough to make those decisions. No matter how you answer that question we as parents need to take a hard look at how we help or fail to help our children set goals and reach them. Goal setting is one of the most important skills we can help our children acquire.

The importance of goal setting for children when it comes to their education is connected to research that shows how disconnected children are from their own academic progress because they are not setting their own goals. Teachers have state and federal guidelines, parents and school boards have specific expectations, so by the time it trickles down to the children there is little emphasis put on the individual goals that the kids might envision. Therefore, without goal setting academic progress becomes less important and more difficult to achieve.

I am thankful that I can place much of the goal setting before my children and have them deeply involved with the directions of their studies. While I am still accountable for certain aspects of their education they are allowed certain latitude for subjects, resources used, and time frames for completion. Instead of entering a classroom where the goal has already been set to finish 80% of the math book by the end of the year, I believe students in the 5th grade should set goals to help improve their writing skills. Once the children were given opportunities for self-direction dramatic improvements were noted. The literature review also revealed what many parents probably already know when children have a vested interest in the outcome they are more motivated and willing to do the work to achieve the end result. Children who learn to set goals develop their self-confidence and increase their abilities to independently find success.

Set and achieve your goals.

Start now when you are young and if you have children train them and keep it simple. For example, a goal for the morning could be to get dressed, eat breakfast, and drive to the library, school, or work. This will help establish the word *goal* into the child's or your vocabulary with easy to reach measurements.

Set good examples by: sharing your own personal goals, how you are attempting to reach, and what obstacles may sometimes get in your way. Define the difference between long-term and short-term goals for you and your kids. Let them know you do not expect them to decide on their career today, but that a long-term goal might own their own business someday and a short-term goal might be finishing their science project by Friday.

Demonstrate how to set mini goals and encourage your children to do the same. Instead of asking them what they want to be in 30 years ask them to make small daily and weekly goals. Finishing a building creation, biking 3 miles a day, or even reading 30 minutes every morning are reasonable goals. Achievable goals help set kids up for success and make it more likely that they will accept new challenges and make new goals.

Do not allow the pattern of quitting to exist within you or your children. If you or your children make a commitment to a project encourage them to see it through to completion even if it is not the journey either of you expected. Allowing kids to quit whenever the going gets tough just reinforces to them that you did not have faith in them to get the job done.

Help your children reach their goals by regularly checking in with them on their progress and offering tools that might help them reach their goals. Make sure you also learn how to define steps within the process that will help them succeed.

Help your children to recognize the value of internal rewards for goal completion. If you offer a toy or money for each goal reached it takes away the value of the task. Children should be encouraged to acknowledge pride in their efforts and as parents we can affirm for them the strength it took them to achieve their goals.

Personal Goal Setting
Planning to Live Your Life Your Way

Many people feel as if they are adrift in the world. They work hard, but they do not seem to get anywhere worthwhile. A key reason that they feel this way is that they have not spent enough time thinking about what they want out of life and have not set formal goals for themselves. Would you set out on a major journey with no real idea of your destination? Probably not!

Goal setting is a powerful process for thinking about your ideal future and for motivating yourself to turn your vision of this future into a reality. The process of setting goals helps you choose where you want to go in life. By knowing precisely what you want to achieve you know where you have to concentrate your efforts. You will also quickly spot the distractions that can so easily lead you away from achieving your goal.

Why Set Goals?

Goal setting is used by top-level athletes, successful business people, and achievers in all fields. Setting goals gives you long-term vision and short-term motivation. It focuses your acquisition of knowledge and helps you to organize your time and your resources so that you can make the very most of your life.

By setting sharp, clearly defined goals, in which you can measure and take pride in the achievement of those goals you will see forward progress in what might previously have seemed a long and pointless grind. You will also raise your self-confidence as you recognize your own ability and competence in achieving the goals that you have set.

Starting to Set Personal Goals

You set your goals on a number of levels:

- First you create your "big picture" of what you want to do with your life (or over the next 10 years) and identify the large-scale goals that you want to achieve.
- Then, you break these down into the smaller and smaller targets that you must hit to reach your lifetime goals.
- Finally, once you have your plan, you start working on it to achieve these goals.

Setting Lifetime Goals

The first step in setting personal goals is to consider what you want to achieve in your lifetime (or at least, by a significant and distant age in the future). Setting lifetime goals gives you the overall perspective that shapes all other aspects of your decision making.

To give a more broad balanced coverage of all important areas in your life try to set goals in some of the following categories (or in other categories of your own, where these are important to you):

Career - What level do you want to reach in your career or what do you want to achieve?

Financial - How much do you want to earn and by what stage? How is this related to your career goals?

Education - Is there any knowledge you want to acquire in particular? What information and skills will you need to have in order to achieve other goals?

Family - Do you want to be a parent? If so, how are you going to be a good parent? How do you want to be seen by a partner or by members of your extended family?

Artistic - Do you want to achieve any artistic goals?

Attitude - Is any part of your mindset holding you back? Is there any part of the way that you behave that upsets you? (If so, set a goal to improve your behavior or find a solution to the problem.)

Physical - Are there any athletic goals that you want to achieve or do you want good health deep into old age? What steps are you going to take to achieve this?

Pleasure - How do you want to enjoy yourself? (You should ensure that some of your life is for you!)

Public Service - Do you want to make the world a better place? If so, how?

Setting Smaller Goals

Once you have set your lifetime goals start setting a five-year plan of smaller goals that you need to complete if you are to reach your lifetime plan.

Then create a one-year plan, six-month plan, and a one-month plan of progressively smaller goals that you should reach to achieve your lifetime goals. Each of these should be based on the previous plan.

Then create a daily **To-Do List** of things that you should do today to work towards your lifetime goals.

At the early stages your smaller goals might be to read books and gather information on the achievement of your higher level goals. This will help you to improve the quality and realism of your goal setting.

Finally review your plans and make sure they fit the way in which you want to live your life.

Leading yourself to your goals

Leadership is an important component of goal accomplishment in every setting. Whether leadership takes place at the office, in the family, profession societies or our nation you have to have leadership to identify the goals that will be sought after, determine the priorities, and the resources to make success occur. Just as organizations need leadership to accomplish goals you need leadership to accomplish your personal goals. Leadership comes from you and you only.

In short, leadership of self-mastery spells the difference between stumbling along in life or succeeding at everything you set your sights on. Achieve self-mastery and everything you undertake in life will be successful, fulfilling, and enjoyable. It is the single most important element to creating what you desire in your professional and personal life.

Self- mastery does not have to be an elusive virtue found only after decades of deprivation and focused meditation. You can begin exercising your self-mastery today through these actions:

Determine that you are in charge of your personal and professional goals.

Self -mastery *is* leadership of self. Are you in charge of yourself or is someone else? You may have a boss or supervisor at the office; however, that individual does not set your personal and professional goals just certain tasks. You set your personal and professional goals. Self-mastery means you never relinquish control of your goal setting. Period!

Take responsibility.

Self-mastery is about responsibility. To effectively master ones self you must take responsibility for everything even when unknown events or crisis erupts. Success in our careers comes about through taking increasing greater levels of responsibility and the same holds true for taking responsibility for setting your personal and professional goals. Self - mastery means you and only you are responsible for the goals you set.

Identify your most important goals today.

Self -mastery is knowing what your most important goals are at all times. What is it that you wish to achieve personally and professionally? There is no other person on this planet that can give you the answer to this question. You are in charge of determining the answer and you have complete responsibility for doing so. In the next post I will cover the method I use for determining my most important goals.

Say what you're going to do and do what you say.

Self -mastery requires alignment between thought, word, and deed. Thinking and saying one thing and doing the opposite will not take you closer to your personal and professional goals. You will bring about what you think and talk about. Therefore, when your goals are set you must be on the lookout for differences between what you are thinking and saying versus what you are doing. Self- mastery means constantly monitoring and removing the differences between thought, word, and deed.

Celebrate the minor triumphs daily.

Self- mastery is a journey of understanding. Primarily understanding that you won't be 100% on every discipline, task, or goal you set for yourself and understanding that you need to reward yourself for making the right decisions that align your thoughts, words, and deeds as you move towards achieving your personal and professional goals.

In all of the reading on successful people I have accomplished self-mastery and it appeared to be the common thread that led these people to reach their goals. Self-mastery will lead you to your personal and professional goals. You simply need to take charge, take responsibility, and move out today.

NOTES: A week of setting goals.

Goals_____
_____
_____
_____

Sunday_____
_____
_____
_____

Monday_____
_____
_____
_____

Tuesday_____
_____
_____
_____

Wednesday_____
_____
_____
_____

Thursday_____

_____

_____

_____

_____

Friday_____

_____

_____

_____

_____

Saturday_____

_____

_____

_____

Accomplishments_____

_____

_____

_____

Are you a hater or a motivator?

Don't let your haters hold you back.

We have all had enemies or so called friends who have stabbed us in the back. These are called "Haters". I too am not immune to haters, drama seekers or the occasional bully! *"Let your haters be your motivators."* When you come across haters in your life let that motivate you to press on and do what you have set out to do.

No matter what you do or how nice you are to them it is always some kind of drama with them. It can be nothing more than pure jealousy; otherwise, why would the person even bother to do or say anything at all. You have the confidence they wish they had. Continue to do all the right things, hold your head high, and always smile.

When you have haters it can mean you are doing something right that they do not like. Keep moving on and reach for the stars. The sky is the limit. Never let anyone hold you back or tell you how you should be. Make your haters your motivators.

Yes, I know we are supposed to be spiritual and most of us are, but we all work differently and have different beliefs because of our own experiences and skills. The psychic world of business is extremely competitive! But think of it in this way because we as psychics make our living by having clients. The more clients we have the more success we have.

The more success the more your actions and words are twisted by others in the media or by others who are jealous. If you are in a similar situation of haters or bullies remember that people do not define who you are, YOU do! People believe what they want to believe. If you are one of the people stuck in the middle of drama and not sure what to believe do not be forced to choose sides. There is always two sides to the story.

1st

Never argue, confront, or struggle with haters. When you engage the hater you give them the power to control and manipulate you.
Wisdom is too high for a fool.
Do not answer fools according to their folly, or you yourself will be just like them.
As a dog returns to its vomit, so fools repeat their folly.

2nd

No matter what the *hater* does or says remember and *practice* The Golden Rule treat them the way you want to be treated despite how they treat you or what they say about you. This can be difficult especially when what they are saying is not the entire truth. But take the high road because they will continue to drown in their own negativity and jealousy and people will begin to see them for who they actually are.

What goes around comes around and you will reap what you sow.

Do not be overcome by evil, but overcome evil with good.

As water reflects the face, so one's life reflects the heart

3rd

Never let haters throw you off your game. *Nothing pleases a hater more than to see you fail.* Focus intently on achieving your goals and being the best you that you can be. Stay positive and look for the good in *every* situation. Think good thoughts! Expect good things.

You will attract into your life the people, ideas, and circumstances that harmonize with your dominant thoughts.

As iron sharpens iron, so one person sharpens another.

Success is the greatest revenge

Never hold back information!

We all know we need each other to accomplish many things in life. If you have what someone else needs for them to succeed please never hold back the information or tools that you possess to help another person reach the top.

That is what we call HATERS, so remember the saying what you make happen for someone else

God make happen for you. So be a blessing if you have the opportunity to do so.

God did not bless us to have it all to ourselves; he blessed us to be a blessing to others. That is a way to win people to Christ. Don't worry if they are already ahead of you or not. Just do what is right.

The reward will come to you. That is why we see other cultures getting ahead because they are not "Haters". They know how to work together until everyone gets what they need.

It could be as small as volunteering, making a phone call, helping through finances, or it could be babysitting. Whatever the need may be, please do it if you can.

NOTES: Who can I motivate?

Goals_____

_____

_____

_____

Sunday_____

_____

_____

_____

Monday_____

_____

_____

_____

Tuesday_____

_____

_____

_____

Wednesday_____

_____

_____

_____

_____

Thursday_____

_____

_____

_____

_____

Friday_____

_____

_____

_____

_____

Saturday_____

_____

_____

_____

Accomplishments_____

_____

_____

_____

Know who you are and who's you are

We need to know who we are and once we figure that out we won't settle for a lot of things in life. Know that no matter what the naysayers say; you are beautiful and you are accepted.

Know that you are secure and be secure about who you are. No matter the size of your good looking body. No matter the length of your hair or the texture, it is what YOU make of it. It starts in the inside; beauty is only skin deep.

Do not let who you are be determined by your skin color, education, the car you drive, or the house you live in. If we let those things define us and a time comes where we lose those things we will lose ourselves.

So when you define who you are you should begin with the inside and move outward that way a person place or thing will not change who you know yourself to be.

We cannot love someone until we love ourselves and to do that you need to know who you are. Then you have the love to love another.

You are Accepted!

You are God's child. **(John 1:12)**

You are Christ's friend. **(John 15:15)**

You have been justified. **(Rom. 5:1)**

You are united with the Lord. **(1 Cor. 6:17)**

You are bought with a price; you belong to God. **(1 Cor. 6:20)**

You are a member of Christ's body. **(1 Cor. 12:27)**

You are a saint. **(Eph. 1:1)**

You have been adopted as God's child. **(Eph. 1:5)**

You have access to God through the Holy Spirit. **(Eph. 2:18)**

You have been redeemed and forgiven. **(Col. 1:14)**

You are complete in Christ. **(Col. 2:10)**

You are Secure

You are free forever from condemnation. **(Rom. 8:1 & 2)**

You are assured all works together for good. **(Rom. 8:28)**

You are free from any charge against you. **(Rom. 8:31-34)**

You cannot be separated from the love of God. **(Rom. 8:35-39)**

You are established, anointed, sealed by God. **(2 Cor. 1:21 &22)**

You are hidden with Christ in God. **(Col. 3:3)**

You are confident that the good work God has begun in me will be perfected. **(Phil. 1:16)**

You are a citizen in Heaven. **(Phil. 3:20)**

You have not been giving a spirit of fear, but of power, love, and a sound mind. **(2 Tim. 1:7)**

You can find Grace and Mercy in time of need. **(Heb. 4:16)**

You are born of God the evil one cannot touch you. **(1 John 5:18)**

You are Significant

You are the salt and light of the earth. **(Matt. 5:13 &14)**

You are a branch of the true vine, a channel of His life. **(John 15:1 & 5)**

You have been chosen and appointed to bear fruit. **(John 15:16)**

You are a personal witness of Christ's. **(Acts 1:8)**

You are God's temple. (1 Cor. 3:16)

You are ministers of reconciliation for God. **(2 Cor. 5:17-21**

You are God's co-worker. **(2 Cor. 6:1) (1Cor. 3:9)**

You are seated with Christ in the heavenly realm. **(Eph. 2:6)**

You are God's workmanship. **(Eph. 2:10)**

You may approach God with freedom and confidence. **(Eph. 3:12)**

You can do all things thru Christ who strengthens you. **(Phil. 4:13)**

Don't settle

Romantic relationships can define a kid's identity and social status and these early relationships can become very dramatic. Too often they can also become abusive. Girls are usually the victims.

They can confuse controlling behavior with signs of affection and are often reluctant to tell their parents, teachers, or even their friends when emotions escalate to violence.

Many adults have difficulties with such behavior too, but often parents don't talk with their children about what to look out for and what to do if it happens. Has this been a problem for you?

Kathy was in high school and really desired the drama/theater background, but found herself in a situation in which she began striving for the ultimate relationship with a football player.

Kathy came from an abusive background as a child, so she was searching for that attention. Kathy sought out what would make her look and appear better than all of her peers. The kind of attention she was searching for through her relationship caused her to spend most of her time on the relationship and less time on the desires of her heart.

For three years, she allowed herself to be in that relationship until it became physically abusive and something she thought she deserved because she had dealt with this type of situation as a child by family members. Kathy also experienced this type of abuse within her school.

Kathy said she ended up feeling like she needed to reach a certain social status, but she also just wanted to be loved, noticed, and accepted. Therefore, her relationship did not feel wrong to her because she had never received those things as a child.

This really was not the direction she wanted her life to go in because of the passion she had for theatre. Consequently, the relationships she chose continued to be the same.

Kathy was asked by one of her peers why she had not shared her past with anyone and she responded by saying; 'I grew up in a really small town and it was one of those things that happened, but was never talked about because no one would have believed me or it would have gotten around town and everyone would have known.

I guess I just did not feel comfortable talking to my parents about it or sharing it with anybody in particular. It did not seem I had an option at that time. I think there was more fear than anything and I think I let that fear take over.

Hiding it seemed like the best option to me along with burying those feelings and emotions deep inside. This way I did not have to deal with it and I could move on with my life and get accepted into college. However, I find myself trapped in this relationship and I almost feel like there is no way to escape.

I sought counseling while I was at college working for a camp and I realized I had people surrounding me that truly cared about me and my well-being. During counseling I found out that living my life in that way and being entrapped by the relationships I chose, as well as the abuse; what I had subjected myself to was not the normal way to live my life.'

Reach high

Of all the failures I have shared with you in this book I still made the choice not to settle for anything less than what God has for me. He told me I do not have to lack any good thing.

The only failure; is the one that does not get back up again. I get up after each fall I took, but I dusted myself off and tried again. It does not mean that I don't have troubles because trust me I do.

Just ask my awesome Pastor (Pastor Blunt) because he says if you do not have any problems I can give you some of mine. I did not settle just because I was raised in the hood; I moved away and made sure that my children would have a better neighborhood than I did. They attend an awesome school district and they have maintained honor rolled status throughout their entire time in school. One of my daughters runs track and has already been told she will be receiving a full athletic scholarship (AMEN).

Furthermore, because I did not settle I know what it feels like to own and operate a family owned convenient store. I also know what it feels like to assist my husband with his construction company.

Just because I grew up in my childhood church did not mean that I had to remain there if I was no longer receiving the word of God to feed my spiritual need. So, now I attend the best church for me and my family (Church on the Rock!), which is the place where we all receive the word and serve.

Lastly, because I did not settle I am now working within the public schools mentoring youth and helping with many other different needs they may have such as: building confidence, self-esteem, providing attire for school proms, and college attire. I have found this to be the best feeling to me. To help the youth is my calling. I have discovered that because I chose not to settle.

My non-profit organization is called City Glamour Girls and Guys! Read more about it at www.cityglamour.org .

NOTES: I AM!

Goals_____

_____

_____

_____

Sunday_____

_____

_____

_____

Monday_____

_____

_____

_____

_____

Tuesday_____

_____

_____

_____

_____

Wednesday_____

_____

_____

_____

_____

Thursday_____

_____

_____

_____

_____

Friday_____

_____

_____

_____

_____

Saturday_____

_____

_____

_____

Accomplishments_____

_____

_____

_____

POEM

If there was ever a time to dare, to make a difference, to embark on something worth doing,

IT IS NOW!

Not for any grand cause, necessarily, but for something that tugs at your heart, something that's your inspiration, something that's your dream.

You owe it to yourself to make your days here count.

HAVE FUN, DIG DEEP, STRETCH, AND DREAM BIG.

Know that things worth doing seldom come easy.

There will be good days and there will be bad days.

There will be times when you want to turn around,

pack it up and call it quits. Those times tell you

that you are pushing yourself, that you are not afraid to learn by trying.

PERSIST.

Because with an idea, determination, and the right tools,

you can do great things.

Let your instincts, your intellect, and your heart, guide you.

TRUST.

Believe in the incredible power of the human mind.

Of doing something that makes a difference.

Of working hard, laughing, and hoping.

Of lazy afternoons, of lasting friends, of all the things that will cross your path this year.

The start of something new brings the hope of something great,

ANYTHING IS POSSIBLE!

Notes

Notes

I will like to thank my mom for doing all she knew how to do. Love You!

Special dedication to my uncle, you always have believed in everything my brother and I wanted to do. Having faith in us, saying 'don't give up, you can do it.' I love you for that… waiting on your return.

Rodney Harvey

www.ingramcontent.com/pod-product-compliance
Lightning Source LLC
Chambersburg PA
CBHW071422040426
42445CB00012BA/1255